# Look at the Lizard

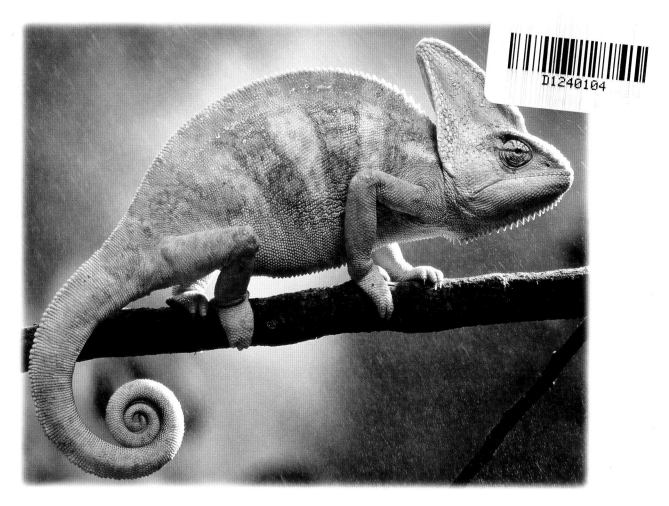

Written by **Ronald James**   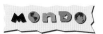   Photograph by **Tim Flach**

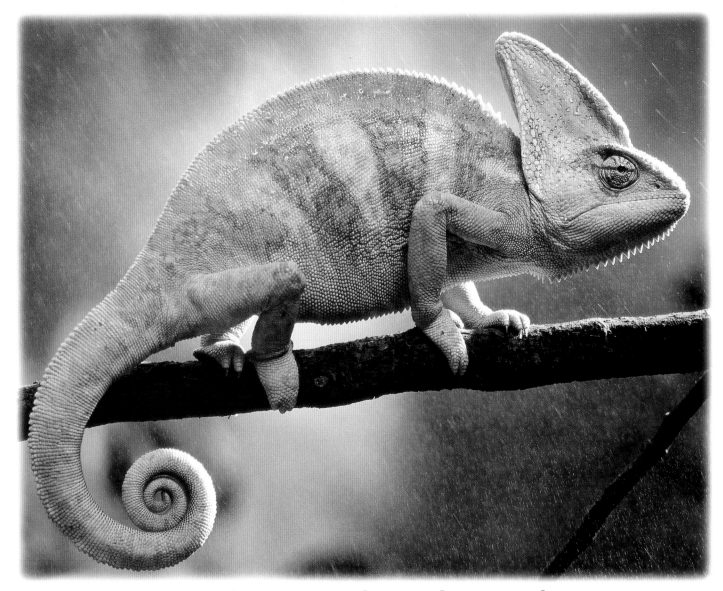

Look at the lizard.

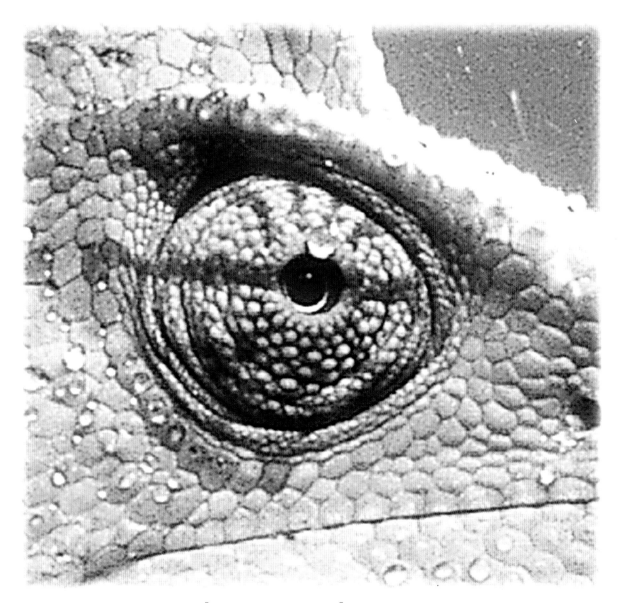

Look at the eye.

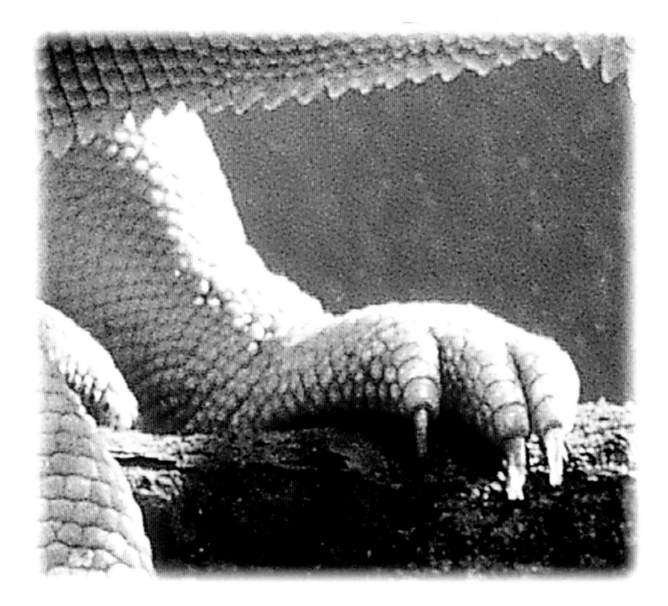

Look at the foot.

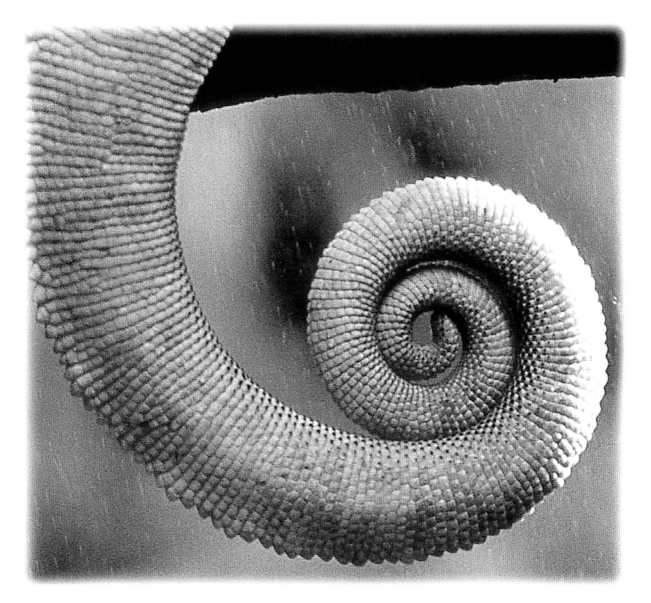

Look at the tail.

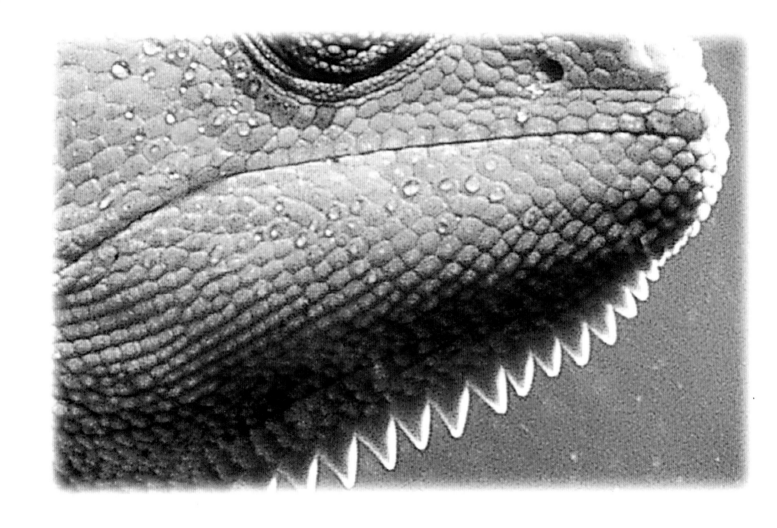

Look at the mouth.

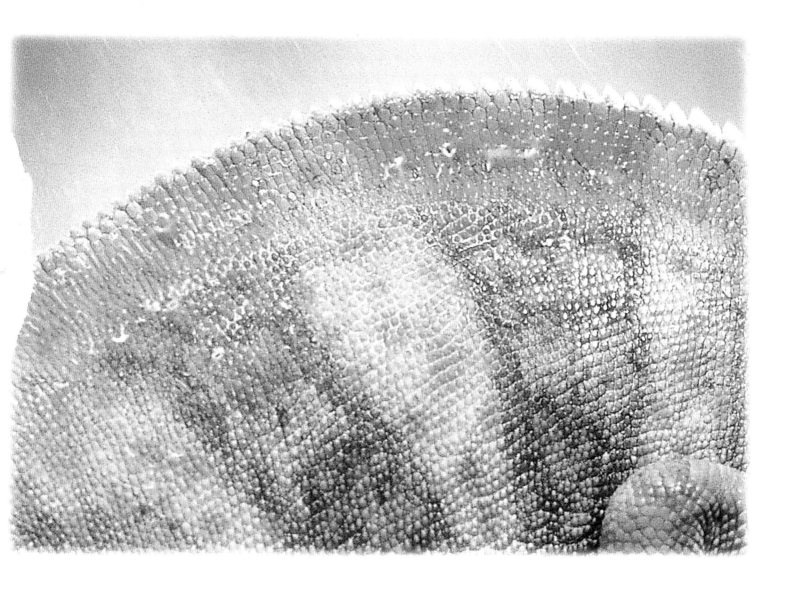

Look at the back.

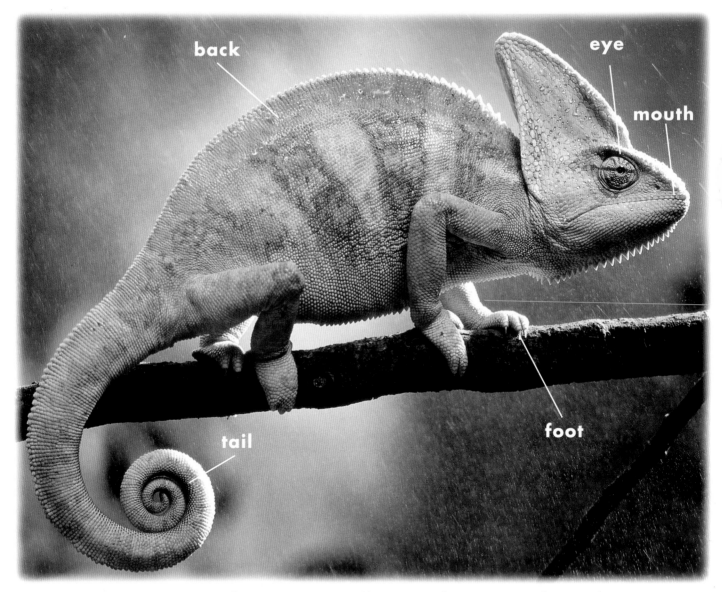

back

eye

mouth

tail

foot

# Look at the lizard!